FORT WAGNER
A SOLDIER'S STORY

Table of Contents

By
MARK W. LESLIE

MARK W LESLIE

FORT WAGNER:
A SOLDIER'S STORY
Copyright © Mark W. Leslie
New Breed Publishing Huntsville AL 2025
First print 2025
Printed by Draft2Digital
ALL RIGHTS RESERVED

This Book is Rated G: General for all ages

NEW
BREED
PUBLISHING
COMICS, MAGAZINES, PAPERBACKS

MARK W LESLIE

Fort Wagner, also known as Battery Wagner,
was a coastal defense fortification,
located on Morris Island, South Carolina,
during the American Civil War.
It played a significant role,
in one of the war's most famous battles:
*The **Battle of Fort Wagner** in 1863.*
The Battle That Changed
Everything.

Prelude:

THE WINDS OF WAR had swept across the United States, tearing at the fabric of the nation. As soldiers from both the Union and Confederate armies clashed across battlefields, a new chapter of courage and sacrifice would be written in the sands of South Carolina.

This is the story of the brave men who fought at **Fort Wagner**, where valor would be tested, where duty would be questioned, and where the very soul of the nation would be forged in the fire of this war.

Once a slave, now a soldier, Tripp—**Private Tripp** was one of many who answered the call when the Union announced the creation of the **54th Massachusetts**.

He was not the first to sign-up nor was he the last, but sign-up he did. He's not really sure why he joined, to save his people from slavery, to save this broken nation, or was it just something to do. At this point of the war, his reasons are not even clear to himself. Although he stands a whopping six feet five inches, he never stood out from the crowd, well not until...

Step-1:
"Up Men, Onto Your Post!"

Present Day 1863 three weeks after the Battle of **Fort Wagner** in a nice sized court house in a small southern town in Tennessee that was taken by the Union army some time ago.

Private Tripp is escorted by two white soldiers inside. They enter the courtroom as he walks toward the bench to take his seat in a single chair positioned in front of the bench which sits three high-ranking officers while other lower ranks sit in the spectators' seats behind where Tripp will be sitting.

Once he takes his set, one-star General Mayfield addresses anyone,

"Welcome to these proceedings. As you all know nearly a month ago the Union army's first colored troop engaged the Confederates in a battle at Wagner, and as many of you know, it didn't go as planned. So we are here to figure out what went wrong and where to point the fingers."

"Speaking for the state will be Colonel Baumhower."

Baumhower stands.

"And speaking with the subject will be Major Albright."

he stands.

"Let us get this hearing started shall we." Lieutenant Curt you may proceed."

He replies, "Yes sir" Curt walks over to Tripp "Stand up private." Tripp stands as Curt has to adjust to seeing such a tall fellow. "Dawn they grow you boys big in the cotton fields."

"Lieutenant!"

"Oh sorry General." Curt turns back to Tripp, "Attention Private." Private Tripp stands at attention, his uniform crisp, his boots polished, but his eyes—those eyes were the windows to the turmoil he carrying within. As he stands in the courtroom, the weight of years and memories fills the space between the words he's about to speak. The lawyer Colonel Baumhower, adjusted his glasses, watching Tripp with keen interest as Curt asks, Tripp "Do you swear to tell the truth the hold truth, and noting be the truth so help you God?"

Tripp answers, "Yes sir."

"Be seated private."

The general says, "Colonel Baumhower you may begin."

Baumhower steps down from the bench and walks toward Tripp to get a real good look at him, with a steady and professional voice he asks, "Private Tripp, please recount for the court the moment the **54th Massachusetts** Infantry took their first steps toward **Fort Wagner**,"

Tripp's lips tightened, and for a moment, he was far away. Far from the clean, cold walls of this military courtroom, back to the heat and dust of the day, the battle began.

The Morning of the Battle:

It was early in the morning on July 18, 1863, the air was thick with anticipation. **The 54th Massachusetts** Infantry had marched for miles, their shoes worn and sweat clinging to their faces, but there was no turning back. The men were lined up in neat formation as they marched passed other units shouts and cheers rigs out

"Give-em hell 54th! give-em hell!"

At that point many of the 54th knew as they approached the rocky beaches of **Morris Island** that there was no turning back now. Ahead of them, rising like a silent, imposing giant, was **Fort Wagner.**

The soldiers stood in silence, but there was a hum in the air, the kind that precedes something monumental. A quiet unease hung like smoke in the air.

Tripp recalls —his nervousness—felt something more. He felt the weight of history if he didn't live up to the standard of a soldier in a fight.

They approached their positions, Private Tripp recalled how "The Colonel, the young officer leading them, rode to the front." His figure was tall and commanding, his eyes steady, though, behind them, there was an undeniable resolve. "He rode his white horse toward the news people and handed a stack of letters he wrote to one of them, asking him to mail them if he should fall this day."

Tripp tells of the two rivals in front of him. One was about to fall but the other grabbed him so he could regain his balance.

"Whatever issue they had was resolved right then".

"The Colonel rode toward us. His boots echoed against the earth as he jumped down from his horse. He raised his hand, everyone stopped moving. Everything was still. The Colonel spoke, his voice cutting through the tension. His voice rang out, strong and sure,

"Men, you are the first of your kind. You are not just soldiers, you are the **embodiment of freedom** and the future of this nation. The world is watching, and we will show them that no man is inferior. We fight not for ourselves, but for those who cannot fight for themselves. You are not here by chance—you are here because the world needs you. We are the 54th. You are brothers."

He points to the flag bearer "If this man should fall? Who will pick up the flag and carry on?"

one soldier steps out saying,

"I will."

We all cheered and the Colonel smiled for this wasn't just any soldier to him, he was the Colonel's childhood friend.

The Colonel who said to the private "I will see you in the fort Tom."

There was a pause before he added with power and conviction,

"Up men, onto your post!"

Back in the Courtroom:

Private Tripp's eyes glazed over slightly as he came back to the present, shaking himself out of his memories. He felt taller now, the courtroom around him fading for a brief moment.

Baumhower breaks the silence.

"Now, tell us private about the moments after that. What happened next after the Colonel's speech?"

Tripp swallowed hard and shifted in his seat, feeling the heavy gaze of the courtroom upon him. He cleared his throat before answering.

"After the speech, sir, we moved out. The air was thick like a storm was brewing. We knew what was coming. We were ready... but nothing can truly prepare you for that kind of fight. Nothing can prepare you for seeing your comrades fall, for hearing the chaos of battle, for feeling the heat of the cannon fire—*nothing*."

Baumhower nodded as he glanced over at the General before asking the next question.

"Private Tripp, did you have any notion of how brutal the battle would be once you reached the Fort?"

Tripp stared ahead, eyes focused on the invisible past, where the smell of gunpowder and the sound of war still lingered in his mind.

"I don't think any of us truly understood until we saw it for ourselves, sir. You know what they say—no battle plan survives contact with the enemy. We were just following orders. But when you see the walls of **Wagner**, and the smoke rising from the cannons... you realize that you're not just fighting for victory anymore. You're fighting for survival."
Baumhower nodded again as he addressed the Albright,
"I yield the floor, you witness major"

he returns to his seat on the bench.

End of Step-1

Step-2:
"The March into Glory: The 1st Charge"

The courtroom was still, the only sounds being the soft shuffle of papers and the occasional cough. **Major Handover Albright** stood to take his turn, his polished uniform cutting a sharp figure against the stark walls of the room. His dark eyes locked in on Private Tripp, his expression unreadable.

Baumhower, having finished his questioning, sat back down, giving a slight nod of disapproval to Tripp, who was still standing tall.

"Private Tripp," Albright began, his voice calm and measured, "you may take your seat." Tripp nodded and carefully lowered himself into the chair, trying his best to keep his composure as the attention of the courtroom shifted to Major Albright.

Albright paced slowly in front of Tripp before coming to a stop. The room held its breath as he folded his hands behind his back and addressed the Private directly.

"Now, Private, I want to ask you a simple question, but one that I imagine has no simple answer. How were you feeling just before charging into battle? What was on your mind?" Albright's gaze never wavered from Tripp's eyes, studying him like a hawk circling its prey.

Tripp paused, his face growing contemplative as he seemed to drift into his thoughts once again. For a moment, the world around him faded. The courtroom disappeared, and he was back on that sun-drenched morning, his feet sinking into the sand, the weight of his rifle heavy in his hands.

"I was scared," Tripp answered, his voice steady but tinged with an honesty that could not be denied.

"A man would be a fool not to be. But there was something else. There was a sense of duty, sir. A belief that we were there for a purpose bigger than ourselves. We weren't just fighting for freedom... we were fighting to prove ourselves. To prove that we were as good as any other soldier. To show that we weren't just **cannon fodder**—we were soldiers, just like the rest of them. But most of all we were **fighting for our people.**"

Albright gave a slight nod, his face impassive but clearly processing Tripp's words.

"Very well," Albright said, moving on. "And then, what happened next? What did you experience when the Colonel gave the order to charge?"

Tripp's hand tightened into a fist at his side as his memories once again carried him back to the battlefield. He swallowed hard, but the images were as clear as day.

The March into Battle:

It was a moment that still burned in his mind—the order. It came from his commanding officer, who had been by their side through thick and thin. Standing tall, his face grim, he raised his hand and gave the command with authority.

"Forward march!"

With those words, it was as if time itself had bent to the colonel's will. The men of the 54th started moving. Tripp's legs seemed to carry him without thinking, and all around him, the soldiers of the 54th were on the move, their boots pounding against the earth.

"We were a sight to see, sir,"

Tripp continued in the courtroom, a slight grin tugging at his lips despite the gravity of the memory.

"The uniforms, the flags... the sound of thousands of boots in unison. It felt like the very ground was shaking beneath us. But it wasn't just the sound or the sight. There was something inside each man, something alive. A sense of pride."

Tripp paused for a moment, he continues.

"But the Colonel wasn't done. He knew what we were up against. So, when we had covered so many yards, he shouted—*"At the double quick!"*

The command echoed in Tripp's mind as though it had been spoken only moments ago. The soldiers quickened their pace, their hearts pounding as they ran faster, the weight of their equipment no longer a burden but a part of them, a part of the charge.

"Then came the final order—

"Double Time!"

Tripp recalled, his voice louder now as he relived that electrifying moment.

"We were sprinting. We were running full tilt, every man doing his best to keep up. The roar of the cannon fire started, and the bullets started to fly overhead, but we weren't going to stop. Not then. Not when we were so close."

Back in the Courtroom:

Albright was nodding, his eyes studying Tripp with an unblinking focus. "And what was it like, Private? Running at full speed towards **Fort Wagner**, knowing what was ahead?"

Tripp exhaled deeply, his hands gripping the armrests of his chair.

"It was like nothing else, sir. It was fear, but it was also something else. It was like running into history, running into **GLORY**. A lot of men would've faltered in that moment. But we—"

He stopped himself, a breath escaping his lips.

"We were doing it for something bigger than ourselves."

"Understood, Private."

Albright paused, his voice dropping slightly.

"And what happened next? What were your first impressions?"

Tripp's face darkened, and the intensity in his eyes became sharp as he prepared to recount the rest of the battle, the fear, and the violence that awaited him, that awaited all of them.

"The Colonel gave the final order to **"Charge!"**

—we did."

End of Step 2

Step 3:
"Cover of Darkness"

The courtroom was quiet for a moment before Colonel Baumhower stood to continue his questioning. His voice was calm but sharp, cutting through the air with practiced precision as he turned toward Private Tripp.

"So, Private,"

Baumhower began, his tone almost sarcastic,

"what happened next after your grand, glorious charge into battle?"

Tripp's mind drifted back to the chaos that had followed the initial rush, the dust, the smoke, the screams, and the sound of gunfire. He could still feel the heat of the day and the weight of his rifle. His hands trembled slightly as he recalled the heat of battle. He straightened in his seat, trying to push aside the haunting memories.

"**Wagner** opened fire on us, sir,"

Tripp said, his voice steady.
"The cannons and mortars from the fort, turned from the US naval ships to fire on us as we charged along the coastline. It was hot and heavy, sir. Shells were exploding all around us, and the air was thick with smoke. It felt like the world itself was coming apart by the seems, sir."

Baumhower leaned forward, his hands clasped in front of him, looking intently at Tripp.

"Just how many men do you think were lost during that initial charge, Private?"

he asked, his voice low and measured, almost with an edge of impatience.

Tripp paused, his eyes darkening as he tried to focus on the question. He swallowed, his mind fighting to suppress the painful memories of the fallen men.

"I can't say for sure, sir,"

Tripp answered, his voice tight.
"There was so much chaos. One moment you'd be running, and the next... men were just gone. Taken by the fire. Or by the water. I couldn't keep track of them all, no one could."

Baumhower raised an eyebrow, not pressing further, but his eyes were filled with a quiet intensity.

"Continue, Private. What else happened?"

Tripp's gaze dropped to his hands as he tried to steady his breathing, the heat of the battlefield once again rising in his chest.

Flashback to the Battle at Wagner:

The day had been relentless, the sun high in the sky as they charged toward the fort's defenses. But soon after the artillery fire started, the Colonel shouted the orders that would lead them into whatever cover they could find.

"Get down! Find whatever cover you can and wait until dark! We will charge again"

His order was given, his voice booming over the roar of the artillery. The men scrambled for cover as explosions shook the ground beneath their feet.

Tripp continued, his voice becoming more distant as the memories flooded back.

Baumhower ask, cover? "What possible cover could be found out in the open field while being fired upon? Utter madness."

Tripp responds,

"Well, sir, we were always told that when the shells start flying, one spot is as good as another. Some of us made it to the enemy's first barriers and hid behind them. Others... well, some of us used our dead buddies as shields. Some of us lay in the Shiloh waters hoping their guns would not point toward the water. Some of us dug into the sand trying to hide, while still others just lay there in the open praying that none of the shells would hit. There wasn't much else we could have done, sir."

Baumhower's expression shifted, his brow furrowing as he leaned in, his voice tinged with disbelief.

"You're telling me you hid behind the bodies of your fallen comrades?"

Tripp's eyes met Baumhower's, unwavering.

"Yes, sir some of us did," he answered simply. "There was no choice. We had to make do with what we had."

Baumhower seemed to mull over this for a moment, then pressed on, his voice heavy, his mouth twisted into a small, almost bitter smile...

"And what about you Private? What did you do for cover? Uh, what did you do?

He asked, his voice steady but his words laced with a touch of derision as if to imply that the question should hold some sort of importance.

Tripp's mind raced again, recalling the many different ways men had tried to survive the firestorm.

Suddenly, Major Albright shot to his feet, his voice firm and commanding as he interjected. "That question is irrelevant, Colonel," he said, his words slicing through the courtroom with precision.

"How a man chose to cover himself under fire should not be in question in these proceedings."

General Mayfield, who had been listening intently, nodded in agreement. "I agree with Major Albright, taking cover when ordered to do so should not question one's valor."

Baumhower explains, "General was trying to make a point of the private's character by seeing how he choose to hide."

Tripp yells with a deep manly voice of authority,

"I did not hide!"

Bam! Bam! Bam!

The gavel sounded as Mayfield spoke loudly,

"Order!" "Order!"

He looks firmly at Tripp, "There will be no more outburst from you private." he also addresses Baumhower, "As for you Colonel. The Private's means of cover is a closed issue, there's no need to focus on the matter any further, so move on. Continue with your questioning, Colonel.."

Baumhower hesitated for a brief moment, his eyes narrowing as he considered the interruption. After a long pause, he simply nodded, the bitterness still apparent in his expression. He then turned back to Tripp, his voice smooth but edged with finality.

"No further questions. Your witness Major."

End of Step-3

Step-4:
"Into Glory: 2nd Charge"

The courtroom remained still, the silence heavy as all eyes turned toward Major Albright, who now stood with an intent focus on Private Tripp. The sound of papers rustling as the court reporter's writing away in the background was the only noise.

Albright's gaze was steady as he nodded for Tripp to continue.

"Private, please, continue your testimony,"

He said, his tone calm but with a hint of authority.

Tripp straightened in his seat, recalling the events of that fateful night, the darkness creeping in as the battle raged around them. He took a deep breath before beginning again.

"Well, sir, once it got dark, the Colonel was ready,"

Tripp began, his voice low as he mentally stepped back into the chaotic night. "He stood up, gave the order to charge, and I,,, we were on our feet again, ready for whatever came next."

Baumhower yells out "Stood up from where Private?!" trying to sneak in a call back to the taking of cover issue.

BAM! BAM!

Mayfield says, "Order! Continue Albright."

Albright turns to Baumhower saying "Please Colonel it's my turn."

Mayfield repeats, "I said continue Major."

Albright turns back to Tripp saying,

"Go on private."

Albright leaned forward, eager for more.

"And then what, Private?"

Tripp paused, his eyes glazed for a moment as the memory rushed back in full force. His voice was steady, but the weight of the recollection showed in his eyes.

"Well, sir, like I said, I stood up to join the charge, and..."

Tripp's words trailed off as Baumhower suddenly interrupted, his voice sharp.

"And what, Private?!"

Baumhower yelled, his patience clearly running thin. Albright turned to Baumhower with a fierce gaze. "Please, Colonel, it's my turn to question," he said, his voice cold but commanding. "Kindly allow the Private to continue."

Baumhower took his seat again, glaring at Albright but refraining from further interruption.

Mayfield whispered, "Easy colonel."

Albright turned back to Tripp, his demeanor softening. "Go on, Private. We're listening."

Tripp nodded, grateful for the moment to continue. "I was amazed at how many of us were still alive, sir," he said, his voice reflecting the wonder of survival amidst the carnage.

"After hours of cannons raining down on us, we only lost a few men. We made it through the worst of it, and I thought, 'Maybe we'll actually make it.'"

Albright's voice was sharp again as he asked the next question, his gaze never leaving Tripp. "And the second charge, Private? What happened?" Tripp's face hardened as the memories came rushing back, his grip tightening on the edges of his chair.

"Well, sir, we ran through all the enemy's outer barricades," Tripp said, his voice rising in intensity as he recalled the adrenaline of the moment.

"The cannons were no longer a problem. We were close. We had made it to the base of the fort itself. That's when things... got crazy."

The courtroom fell into a tense silence as Tripp's words hung in the air. Albright, his expression unwavering, gave a slight nod.

"That's all for now, Private. No further questions."

End of Step-4

Step-5:
"Fire from Above"

The tension in the courtroom was palpable as Colonel Baumhower stood up from his seat, his polished boots clicking sharply against the floor. He walked toward Private Tripp, eyes narrowing as he stopped just a few feet away. The room fell into complete silence.

Baumhower's voice was calm but with an edge, like a blade ready to strike.

"You said you all made it to the base of the fort, Private. What then?" He asked, his tone probing.

Tripp leaned forward in his seat, his hands clasped together tightly. The weight of the question was heavy, but he was prepared to relive it. His voice broke the silence as he answered.

"Well, sir, the sides of the walls slope at an angle, and the enemy was all along the top, shooting down on us,"

Tripp eyes distant as he recalled the onslaught.

"We were pinned down. Some of us shot back, but I don't think we were winning that exchange."

Baumhower's eyes hardened as he crossed his arms.

"And, Private, what happened next?"

Tripp took a deep breath, his chest tightening with the memory.

"The Colonel grabbed hold of the flag bearer, and they stood up, running at the Rebs,"

He said, his voice tinged with sorrow at the recollection.

Baumhower's expression remained unreadable, but he pressed on.

"Well?"

Tripp's gaze dropped to the floor, the weight of the moment still fresh in his mind. His voice softened.

"Well, sir... they were shot. Both of them."

The courtroom remained still, the words hanging in the air like a pall over the room. Albright's face betrayed no emotion, but there was a slight clench in his jaw.

Baumhower, however, did not flinch. Instead, he took a step back, returning to his seat. Saying,

"No further question, your witness Major."

Baumhower sits down, his eyes now tinged with even more disdain. He thinks,

"Dam it."

End of Step-5

Step-6:
"Over the Top"

The courtroom remained heavy with the weight of the earlier testimony. Private Tripp's words still hung in the air, and the room seemed to draw in on itself. Colonel Albright stood, his gaze never leaving Tripp as he prepared to continue the questioning.

Alright addresses, "Private."

Albright began, his voice stern but steady.

"What happened after the Colonel was killed?"

Tripp's posture stiffened as the memory hit him hard, but he pressed forward.

"Well sir, we followed his last orders."

Albright asks, "Order? What last order?"

Tripp answers,

"Will, when the colonel ran toward the Rebs he yelled,

"Come on 54th!"

It caused a massive rally, sir."

He recalled.

"Private Samms grabbed the flag, turned back at us yelling,

'COME ON!'

So we charged upward. It was a sight to see, sir."

Before Albright could respond, Baumhower's voice rang out sharply. "A sight to see, huh?"

General Mayfield immediately raised his hand. "Order!" he barked. "Major, continue your questioning."

Albright gave a brief nod before he turned back to Tripp.

"What happened next?" he asked, eyes sharp as he awaited his answer.

Tripp swallowed hard before continuing.

"Many of us made it to the top, sir. We fought hand to hand. Some of us broke through their line."

Albright's gaze sharpened.

"What happened to Samms?"

He pressed, his tone more insistent now.

Tripp hesitated, the memory of Samms's final moments flashing in his mind.

"He went down a few seconds after yelling for us to come on, I never saw Private 1st Class Samms again,"
he said quietly.

Baumhower could no longer contain himself.
"What about the ones that broke through? What happened to them?"
he demanded.

Tripp looked Baumhower directly in the eyes, his voice tinged with frustration.

"I don't know, sir,"
He replied, his shoulders slumping slightly.
"I reached the top, killed a Reb, then I was shot in the shoulder. I fell all the way back to the base of the fort... Sir!"

A hushed murmur spread through the courtroom at Tripp's words.

Albright walked over to Tripp, placing a hand on his non-injured shoulder as a sign of respect. He then turned to Baumhower, his voice firm.

"No further questions, Your witness Colonel"
Albright said, his eyes locking with Baumhower's for a moment before he took a step back.

Baumhower stood in silence, glaring at Tripp, but said nothing as voices from the courtroom started to chatter, whisper, with questions being asked.

End of Step-6

Step-7:
"The Retreat"

The air in the room had grown heavy with tension as the people continued to chatter until...

BAM! BAM! BAM!

"I will have order in this court!" Mayfield barked.

As Private Tripp's story unfolds the details are raw, and the truth of the battle weighs on everyone present, but the hater Baumhower remains unfazed, his gaze steady as he looks at Tripp, awaiting the next part of the story.

He stood tall, his voice cold and calculated as he began,

"After you were shot, and fell back, how long did
you lay down? What else happened, soldier?"

Tripp's eyes grew distant as he recalled the events, his mind taking him back to the battlefield.

"I don't know,"

He said quietly.

"When I opened my eyes, I saw the only white officer to make it out
alive—Captain Lake."

Major Albright spoke up, his voice cutting through the tension.

"Yes, **Captain Lincoln Lake** is the sole surviving officer of the 54th. He's
currently the acting commander until the 54th gets refitted."

Baumhower turned sharply to Albright, his face unflinching.

"Thank you, Major, for your intel on the situation.
"Now back to you, Private,"

He said, with such an icy tone.

"What was Captain Lake doing?"

Tripp swallowed hard, the memory of Lake standing over him coming into focus.

"He was the one that ordered the retreat,"

He answered.

"All the ones that were left fell back. Private Gunn grabbed the flag, while
Privates Luck and Branch both grabbed me. That's all I remember from the
fight, sir."

Baumhower's eyes locked onto Tripp's, searching for something more, something deeper, but found nothing. Tripp's face remained resolute, steady in his testimony.

The silence hung heavy as Baumhower looked over at General Mayfield. "No further questions,"

He said, his voice low and deliberate.

The General gave a slight nod, and the room seemed to settle in the wake of Tripp's words.

End of Step-7

Step-8:
"At the Field Hospital"

Albright rose from his seat, standing tall and imposing. His voice broke the silence as he turned toward Tripp, the final questions about to be asked.

"Private, take us back to the field hospital."

Tripp shifted uncomfortably in his chair, his thoughts distant as the memories came flooding back. His voice was quieter this time as if the weight of his words were too much to bear.

"Well sir, I blacked out, and by the time I woke up, I was in the hospital, they had already taken the bullet out of my shoulder."

Albright leaned in, his tone sharp.

"After you woke up, what did you do next?"

Tripp hesitated. His face grew darker, reluctant to speak, but Albright pressed again.

"What did you do, Private?"

Tripp's lips parted, but before he could answer, Albright interrupted, his voice rising with an edge of frustration.

"I'll tell you what he did!"

Albright gestured sharply toward Tripp, anger flaring in his eyes.

"This man, after he fought in the battle after a bullet was removed from his shoulder, after being told to lay down and rest, after being told to return to his unit... he refused to leave the hospital. He stayed, doing whatever he could to aid the doctors, and the nurses, caring for the men whose injuries were much worse than his!

He aided all the men that were fighting for their lives in that field hospital, black and white soldiers."

The room grew tense as Albright's eyes narrowed on Tripp, challenging him with his words.

"Now tell the court, why would you do that, Private?"

Baumhower shot up from his seat, his voice booming,

"Yes, why would you do that?"

Mayfield, ever the calming presence, interjected, his voice cutting through the rising storm.

"Order, Colonel, we're all ears, Private. Why would you do that?"

Tripp took a deep breath, his chest rising as he prepared to speak the truth that had been sitting heavy in his heart. He looked up at them all, his voice steady and somber. He stands up as a man, not a soldier

"I lost a lot of my friends already during the fight. I had to try to save as many of my friends... I, we had left, and I had to help the other as well. It's what a soldier should do, it's what a man would do,,, sir."

The silence in the courtroom was thick as if every soul present felt the weight of Tripp's words. Albright was the first to break it, his voice rising with passion, fury in his tone.

"Did you hear that?!"

"This soldier this man did his duty and fought the enemies of his country, then this man did his duty to help save the lives of his fellow man! I say to you all in this courtroom—this is the kind of soldier, the kind of man, this army needs! More than any other!"

Albright paused, looking around at the men in the room, his gaze hard.

"I have no further questions."

He turned toward Tripp, placing a hand on his shoulder as he added,

"On behalf of Private Tripp of the 54th Massachusetts, I—we rest General."

Baumhower stood up, his voice carrying the weight of duty and authority.

"On behalf of the United States Army, I too rest General."

Mayfield, looking to calm the escalating tension, raised his hand and spoke with a finality that rang out in the room.

"Let us take a 20-minute recess to compare notes. Court dismissed."

End of Step-8

Step-9:
"Final Deliberation"

THE COURTROOM fell into an uneasy silence, the tension in the air once again palpable. General Mayfield's voice cut through it, calm and commanding as he addressed Private Tripp.

"Private Tripp."

Tripp, standing before the court, straightened up, the weight of the moment heavy on his shoulders. He nodded, acknowledging the General's call.

"Yes, sir."

Mayfield continued, his voice steady but inquisitive.

"Do you have anything you want to add to your testimony?"

Tripp hesitated for a moment, his mind running through everything that had transpired. Then, he spoke with a hint of uncertainty in his voice.

"Well, sir, I'm not sure of the crime I did or the rules I've broken, so I'm not clear on what punishment I'll be getting."

Before anyone could respond, Colonel Baumhower's voice cut through the air with an authoritative edge.

"Stop right there, Private."

The room grew even more still as everyone turned to Baumhower, the gravity of his words catching the attention of all present.

Baumhower turned toward General Mayfield, his posture rigid.

"General, may I continue?"

Mayfield gave a small nod.

"Please, Colonel."

Baumhower stood tall, his voice commanding.

"Private Tripp, you are not up on charges. This is not a trial, but a hearing. It is to understand what truly happened at **Fort Wagner**. We've questioned every survivor, including Captain Lincoln Lake, and asked them to list who all they thought should receive medals for their actions. You, Private Tripp, are the only living member of your unit who has been voted to receive a medal."

The words hung in the air, the significance of the statement sinking in. Tripp's eyes widened slightly as he tried to absorb the news.

Baumhower paused, his gaze locking with Tripp's.

"So, alongside your fallen comrades, you too are awarded the **Medal of Honor**."

Tripp stood frozen for a moment, the reality of it sinking in. The Medal of Honor. A recognition of his actions, of everything that had happened during the battle.

General Mayfield nodded, his voice soft yet firm.

"Albright, would you please read the private his sentence."

Major Albright stood up, holding a piece of paper with the official sentence, and began to read in a clear, formal tone.

"Private Tripp, you are hereby awarded the Army's newest medal the Medal of Honor and in addition you are also here-by sentenced to the rank of First Sergeant with all the rights and privileges of that rank. Congratulations, First Sergeant Tripp."

Tripp was taken aback by the honor, his voice faltering.

"I don't know what to say.

When do I go back to the 54th?"

General Mayfield gave him a look of understanding, his voice now tinged with a sense of finality.

"You don't, Private. Your new assignment is to report to your new commanding officer and serve as his top sergeant with the **5th Regiment Buffalo Soldiers** of the **58th Minnesota Cavalry**.

I hope you can ride a horse, Sergeant. Good luck."

Tripp stood still for a moment, processing the shift in his life. He saluted the officers in the room, his heart pounding with the weight of the change.

The officers, in turn, stood and returned the salute with respect.

General Mayfield gave a nod, the command is final and authoritative.

"Dismissed, Sergeant."

As Tripp turned to leave the courtroom, a new chapter in his life was unfolding. A chapter of honor, duty, and service—far from his home with the **54th**, but a soldier, nonetheless.

End of Step-9

Epilogue -
"Captain Buffalo"

First Sergeant Tripp stood in front of Major Albright's office, waiting for his summons. After a long silence, the door opened, and Albright waved him in.

"You've been called up to meet your new commanding officer, Sergeant,"
he said, gesturing for Tripp to enter.

Tripp straightened his posture, ready to meet yet another white officer. But as he stepped into the office, he was taken aback by the sight of an imposing black man behind the desk. For a moment, Tripp froze, momentarily lost for words. This was a rare sight, as he hadn't expected to meet a black officer, let alone one with such an authoritative presence.

The man stood up from behind the desk, his stature towering at least three inches above Tripp. His uniform was crisp and impeccable, a captain's insignia gleaming on his shoulder.

The officer gave him a slight grin and extended his hand.

"I'm Captain Buffalo. No salutes here, Sergeant. Not until we've earned each other's respect. And I think that's something we'll do as a team, yes?"

Tripp quickly snapped out of his surprise and saluted, but the captain waved it off.

"None of that right now, Sergeant. You're to be my right-hand man, my partner. We're going to need to communicate as equals. No need for all that formality between us. I'm the only black officer in the Union Army, but that doesn't matter. We're both here to lead, and we're going to do just that."

"Captain Buffalo."

Tripp said, taking a moment to steady himself. He had never seen anyone quite like the captain. The man stood at least 6'8", maybe more—taller than anyone Tripp had encountered in the army, or anywhere else.

Tripp had always been the one other's had to looked up to with his height of 6'5', but this man? He had to look up at him, and it was a strange feeling. Tripp shook his head. He'd been in awe, and he knew it.

"Sorry, sir,"

Tripp muttered,

"I didn't mean to stare. I just... wasn't prepared."

Captain Buffalo smiled the look of understanding in his eyes.

"I've seen that look before, Sergeant. Don't worry about it. I'll sure you're ready to work with me, though, on a personal level. You're here now, and we're going to move forward together."

Tripp nodded, taking the captain's words to heart.

"Sir, I've been stationed in the east most of my time in this war, but I thought things were winding down out west."

Captain Buffalo grinned, his eyes glinting with the promise of the mission ahead.

"You thought the war out west was over? Well, not just yet, Sergeant. Have you heard of

Captain Little Rock?"

Tripp frowned, unsure of the name.

"No, sir."

The captain leaned in, his voice lowering.

"Little Rock is a Confederate leader causing trouble in Arkansas. He's been giving our boys out there hell for far too long. It's time we bring the hammer down. I need you with me, Sergeant. We've got a mission: our regiment, and the 58th Minnesota, is headed westward. And we'll deal with Little Rock and his rebels once and for all."

Tripp could hardly believe what he was hearing. "Sir, that's quite the mission. But how are we supposed to pull this off? We've only just formed right?."

Buffalo nodded.

"That's right. We're green, Sergeant. A fresh unit and we'll need to train them along the way. It's going to be rough, but I want you ready for what's to come. We can't waste time. Once we reach Arkansas, we'll be fighting for our survival and for this war to end the right way. Are you up for it?"

Tripp stood straighter, his resolve firming up. "Yes, sir. You can count on me."

"Good then,"

Captain Buffalo said, his smile widening.

"Welcome to the 5th Buffalo Regiment.

Let's show them how it's done."

Tripp grinned and shook the captain's hand again, feeling the weight of the future ahead of him. The mission was far from over, but with Captain Buffalo leading the way, Tripp felt ready for whatever comes next.

And with that, the two men stood, side by side, as they prepared to ride westward together, ready to face the challenges ahead.

End of Epilogue.

Cast

1. **Private Tripp** – The central character, a soldier in the **54th Massachusetts**, who survives the **Battle of Fort Wagner** and is later honored with the Medal of Honor.
2. **The Colonel** – The commanding officer of the 54th Massachusetts, who leads the charge during the Battle of Fort Wagner and is killed in action.
3. **Colonel Baumhower** – A member of the court questioning Private Tripp about the battle.
4. **Major Albright** – Another officer who questions Tripp during the military court hearing.
5. **General Mayfield** – The head of the military court proceedings who oversees the questioning and ultimately renders the decision on Tripp's fate.
6. **Captain Lincoln Lake** – The sole surviving officer of the 54th Massachusetts, who orders the retreat during the battle.
7. **Private Samms** – A soldier in the 54th who grabs the flag after the Colonel's death and leads the charge.
8. **Private Gunn** – A fellow soldier who helps carry the flag during the retreat.
9. **Private Branch** – Another soldier who helps carry Tripp during the retreat.
10. **Private Luck** – Part of the group that carries Tripp after he's wounded.
11. **Flag Bearer** – The soldier who originally carries the flag before being killed.

Mid-Credit:
"The Patriot"

The night was thick with storm clouds, a constant rumble of thunder echoing across the darkened forest. The air was electric, charged with the tension of an impending battle, yet this was no ordinary fight. This was the quiet battle of intelligence and survival.

A masked figure watched from the shadows, his keen eyes fixated on the British rider moving swiftly through the storm-soaked landscape.

The rider, spurred on by the urgency of his mission, urged his horse onward with every ounce of strength. He was delivering crucial intelligence from one British unit to another, but fear gnawed at him—fear of a figure whispered about in the taverns, on the streets, and in the barracks of the British army.

Stories of a man in blue, his face hidden by a mask, riding a ghostly white steed, moving like an avenging specter. That specter, the ghost of American vengeance, had haunted the British soldiers' nightmares for months.

The rider's breath quickened, and his eyes darted nervously over his shoulder, his heart racing with every beat. He could feel the thundering hooves getting closer, the rider of the white horse closing in fast. A chill ran down his spine.

In the distance, lightning flashed, briefly illuminating the path ahead. And then, as if the storm itself had conjured him from the ether, the figure emerged from the shadows.

The masked man, clad in blue, rode hard and fast, his white horse a blur against the dark backdrop of the storm. The rider's blood ran cold with fear as the chase began. He urged his horse faster, the reins snapping in his hands, But it was no use.

The masked rider was gaining on him with an eerie speed, closing the distance in mere moments.

A crack of thunder echoed through the storm just as the British rider's horse stumbled. The man lost his grip and fell to the ground, the bag of letters slipping from his grasp. He scrambled to recover, but the cold, terrifying presence of the masked man loomed over him.

The lightning flashed again, casting a bright silhouette of the mysterious figure standing tall, his body framed by the storm's fury. The British soldier's eyes widened in terror as the man reached down, grabbing the leather pouch of letters with a swift and practiced motion.

The masked man spoke, his voice cold, unwavering:
"Tell your Generals they will not win this war, and to leave my country or you will all die."

The soldier's breath caught in his throat. Fear surged through his veins, his hands trembling as he looked up at the ghostly figure before him. Lightning cracked across the sky, casting brief, jagged shadows.

"Sir... What be thy name?"

The words came out in a whisper, desperate.

The man paused, his eyes glinting under the mask, before he slowly turned toward his horse. His cloak billowed in the wind as he looked back at the fallen rider.

The masked man's voice was a cold promise,

"The Patriot."

The storm seemed to be still for a moment, the echoes of the thunder drowned in the presence of the masked avenger. With that, the Patriot turned and rode into the storm, vanishing like a ghost into the darkness.

The British soldier lay trembling on the wet ground, knowing that the legend of The Patriot was not a tale to be dismissed, but a reality he would never forget.

End of Mid-Credit.

New Breed Ratings Chart

To insure our readers safe enjoyment, and peace of mind for parents as well we here at New Breed Publishing will be rating our books from here forward for your convenience and protection. Below is our standard Ratings Chart

G: General for all ages
PG: Parental guidance
PG-13: May be inappropriate for under 13
M: Mature Readers
R: Restricted parents are advised
RR: Very Restricted Strongly advised
RRR: May be to Harsh for even Mature readers

FORT WAGNER: A SOLDIER'S STORY

Check out some of the other Titles by New Breed Publishing... Out Now

Shadow When Evil Walks (Season Edition)

DARKNESS LOOMS IN THE city that never sleeps which threatens the lives of its citizens, and the only ones who can stop it don't even know what they are truly dealing with. But with the aid of a mystery man, New York's Finest is ready to serve and protect the people. The only questions are "Can they?" and "Just how far they're willing to go?" For When Evil Walks, death follows.

Night on the Haunted Highway

SEVEN COLLEGE STUDENTS head for the beach for spring break. On their travels, they take a pit stop in a small town. Although the locals warned them of the dangers on Route 166 at night... Well, you know how youngster are. So now they must spend a "Night on the Haunted Highway" Who knows what horrors they may run into.

Project Day Break

THREE YOUNG TROOPERS fresh out of boot camp find themselves a mystery, which may hold their base in the balance. Can they save Fort Sun Rise? Let's hope so cause they're all we got.

CODE NAME: AXEL

Raised, and trained by one of the world's most notorious assassin clans, sold off to be an agent and secret weapon for the US. She's out to prove that she's the most lethal killer on this Rock, not only must she take on America's enemies, but she must also battle with inner demons of her own. Demons who are determined to break her... We'll see.

FORT WAGNER: A SOLDIER'S STORY

Mark Jericho: The President's Daughter

EXILING HIMSELF FOR his pasted failure, and haunted by it as well, he's now giving a second chance to make things right. Not only can he save his sanity, he can save a little girl as well. For the last few years our government has been searching for him, the Feds finally found him, and just in time too... Mark Jerimiah Jericho "The Living Wall" is back!

Coming Soon:
Doctor Savannah: Book of Kings
Shadow: Chronicles of Evil
The REAP
Dirk Dangerfield: Daring Man of Mystery
Gregory Beck: Rouge Agent

Post-Credit:

"Captain Little Rock"

The Confederate camp in Arkansas was a flurry of movement as dusk descended. The air was thick with the smoke of campfires, and the sound of troops preparing for the night echoed across the tents. At the center of it all, inside a large, dimly lit command tent, sat **Captain Christopher Carson**, known to all as **Captain Little Rock**. His reputation had grown in the Southern army—his tactics were bold, cunning, and always unpredictable.

Today was no exception. **Lieutenant Michael Marv**, a young, eager officer, stood beside him, grinning ear to ear.

"Once again, Captain, you ran circles around them Yankees! Yes, sir, they didn't know what hit 'em!"

Top Sergeant Flakes, his face as grizzled as they come, nodded in agreement. "Yes, sir, you did it again—turned what should have been a defeat into another Confederate victory."

The other lieutenants—**Pepper**, **Nutt**, and **Knight**—all chimed in with their own, laughter and praise, all too eager to bask in the glory of yet another triumph under Captain Little Rock's leadership.

But Carson, ever humble and focused, waved off their exuberance. He was a man of few words, his actions speaking louder than any victory speech.

"Alright, we need to break camp before those Blue Coats recover," He said flatly, his voice calm and collected.

"Let's move, gentlemen."

He turned toward the canvas flaps of the tent, his boots making a soft thud on the floorboards.

The officers, still filled with pride, followed his command with a shared sense of accomplishment. One by one, they exited the tent, making their way to their respective posts. Their laughter and banter faded as they joined their troops, preparing to march once again.

But as the last of the officers disappeared into the camp, the air grew eerily still.

A ghostly figure materialized from the shadows, appearing as if from thin air. His form was a vague silhouette—an ethereal figure draped in a gray cloak, face obscured by a shadow, his eyes gleaming with an unnatural light.

"You've outdone yourself this time, Captain," the ghost's voice was low, smooth, and chilling as it echoed in the tent. Little Rock, unfazed by the apparition, turned to face the figure.

"Thanks to you, ghost. Your ability to gather information unseen has once again proven to be the difference in this battle. Keep it up like this, and we'll win this war."

The figure chuckled softly, a cold, haunting sound that seemed to carry with it the weight of countless battles.

"Of course, Captain. You can always depend on me. The Gray Ghost..."

The ghost's voice trailed off, his laughter rising in a spine-tingling crescendo as if mocking the very notion of defeat. Little Rock stared at the ghost with a quiet, calculating gaze, his lips curling into the faintest of smiles.

"I always can, Gray Ghost. Let's keep it that way."

And with that, the ghostly figure dissolved into the shadows, leaving Little Rock alone in the tent, his focus returning to the task at hand.

The captain turned and exited the tent, joining his men to prepare for the next stage of their campaign. The war was far from over, but with allies like the **Gray Ghost**, Little Rock knew that the Confederacy had a fighting chance—if only in the shadows.

End of Post-Credit.

First Sergeant Tripp

FULL NAME: Tripp (no known last name)

MARK W LESLIE

Nickname(s): "Big Tripp," "Ironback" (used by fellow soldiers)

Role: Main Protagonist

Affiliation: Union Army → 54th Massachusetts Infantry → 58th Minnesota Cavalry (Buffalo Soldiers)

Historical Setting: American Civil War (1863), Battle of Fort Wagner

Status: Active Duty (Promoted)

Rank:

- **Beginning:** Private
- **Post-Wagner:** First Sergeant

⟨?⟩⟨?⟩ BASIC PROFILE

- **Age:** 24

- **Height:** 6'5"

- **Weight:** 215 lbs

- **Build:** Towering, powerful shoulders, long arms; visibly strong but lean from war life.

- **Complexion:** Deep brown, weathered from sun and stress

- **Eyes:** Intense dark brown – often described as carrying years of pain

- **Hair:** Short, cropped tight, sometimes covered by a cap

- **Facial Hair:** Thin chin beard or stubble (period-accurate)

⚔ BACKSTORY

- **Born into slavery** in the South; separated from family at a young age

- Escaped shortly before enlistment

- **Joined the 54th Massachusetts** not entirely out of patriotism—but because it *felt like the only move left that had meaning.*

- Struggles internally with the idea of fighting for a country that had once enslaved him

- Keeps to himself but is **deeply loyal** to those he respects

◈ PERSONALITY

Trait
Description

Reserved Speaks little unless necessary; thinks before he acts.

Honorable Follows his own strict moral compass—will not abandon a brother-in-arms.

Haunted Carries survivor's guilt and emotional trauma from combat.

Defiant Will *not* be humiliated or broken—stands tall even when accused.

Observant Often notices more than he lets on, reads people well.

Protector Will step in for others, especially the younger soldiers.

◇ NOTABLE QUOTES

- "I did not hide."

- "I don't know if I joined to save this country or just to do *something*, but I fought, and that's all I got left."

- "We weren't fighting for medals... we were fighting so the world couldn't ignore us anymore."

- "I had to help the ones who were still breathing. That's what a soldier should do. That's what a man would do."

⬦ SKILLS & ABILITIES

Category
Details

Combat Skilled in bayonet fighting, trench warfare, close-quarters combat
Leadership Natural leader under fire—respected by men without needing rank
First Aid Learned field bandaging and wound care during his time in the field hospital
Horse Riding Learns quickly (for upcoming cavalry arc in the 58th)
Resilience Endured wounds, battlefield trauma, and systemic racism without breaking

◈ MEDALS & HONORS

- **Medal of Honor** – Awarded for bravery, survival, and leadership during and after the Battle of Fort Wagner

- **Promotion to First Sergeant** – For valor and exceptional conduct post-battle

- **Assigned to Special Service** – Selected to serve under the only Black officer in the Union Army at the time

Here are some key details:

THE BATTLE OF FORT *Wagner*

FORT WAGNER: A SOLDIER'S STORY

1. **Construction and Purpose: Fort Wagner** was built by the Confederacy to defend the port of Charleston, South Carolina, which was a crucial strategic point for both sides. The fort was constructed of sand and earth, giving it a strong defensive position.

2. **The Battle of Fort Wagner (July 18, 1863):** The fort gained prominence during the Second Battle of Fort Wagner in July 1863. Union forces, under the command of General Quincy A. Gillmore, sought to capture the fort to weaken the Confederate hold on Charleston. The battle is most famous for the heroism of the **54th Massachusetts Infantry Regiment**, one of the first **all-Black regiments** in the Union Army, led by **Colonel Robert Gould Shaw.**

Despite their bravery, the assault on the fort was unsuccessful. The Union forces faced heavy resistance from the entrenched Confederate defenders, and the Union troops were forced to retreat after suffering significant casualties.

1. **The 54th Massachusetts Infantry:** The 54th Massachusetts was one of the first **Black American regiments** to fight in the Civil War, and their assault on **Fort Wagner** was a pivotal moment in the war and for **Black American** military service. Colonel Shaw was killed during the battle, and his body was buried with his soldiers in a mass grave, which was later a symbol of the bravery of the **Black soldiers.**

2. **Aftermath:** After the failed assault, the Union forces continued their siege of the fort. However, due to the heavy losses and the difficulty of the assault, the Union eventually decided to lay siege to the fort rather than attempt another direct assault.

3. **The Fort's Fall:** After months of continued shelling, **Fort Wagner** eventually fell in **September 1863**, but by then, Charleston was still heavily defended. The Union forces would go on to blockade the city and continue their attempts to capture it throughout the war.

46

FORT WAGNER: A SOLDIER'S STORY

Fort Wagner is often remembered for its symbolism in terms of courage, sacrifice, and the importance of the **54th Massachusetts** in the fight for **Freedom and Equality**.

If you're looking for more detailed accounts or specific aspects of the 54th Massachusetts and the Battle of Fort Wagner.

◈ Books

1. *A Brave Black Regiment* by Luis F. Emilio

• Written by a veteran of the 54th, this firsthand account is one of the most detailed and revered sources on the unit.

2. *Lincoln and the Negro* by Benjamin Quarles

• Offers context about Black troops in the Union army and Lincoln's evolving policy.

3. *Forged in Battle: The Civil War Alliance of Black Soldiers and White Officers* by Joseph T. Glatthaar

• In-depth analysis of the relationships within units like the 54th.

4. *Lay This Laurel* by Lincoln Kirstein (with photographs by Richard Benson)

• A visual and narrative tribute to the 54th and the Shaw Memorial.

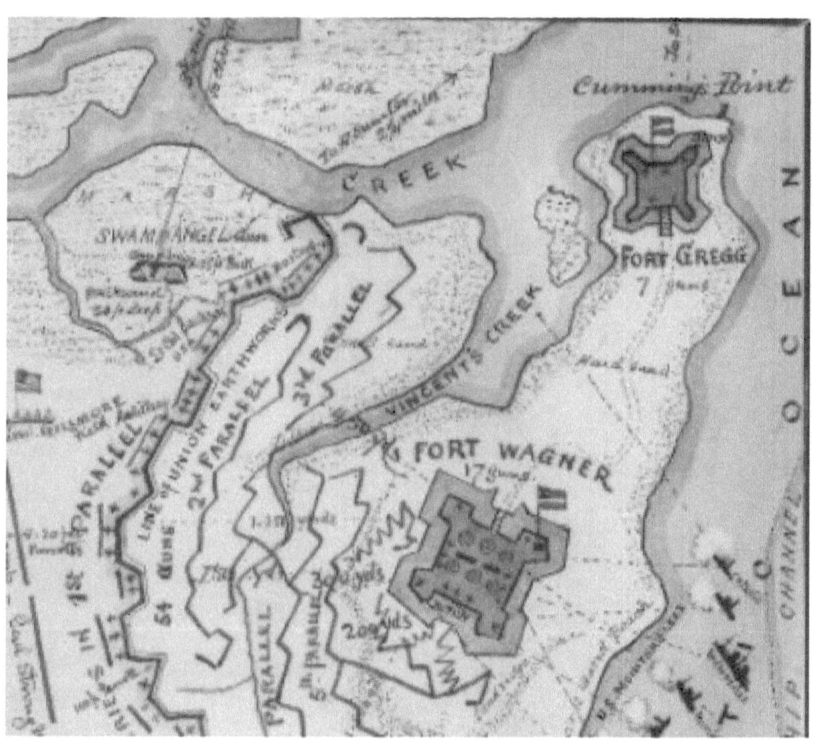
Cummings Point
FORT GREGG
7 guns
OCEAN
CREEK
MARSH
SWAMP ANGEL battery
VINCENT'S CREEK
FORT WAGNER
LINE UNION EARTHWORKS
3rd PARALLEL
2nd PARALLEL
1st PARALLEL
5th PARALLEL
CHANNEL

◈ Websites & Online Databases

1. **National Park Service (NPS)**[1]

• Search for **"54th Massachusetts"** or **"Fort Wagner"** for battlefield maps, articles, and historical context.

2. **American Battlefield Trust**[2]

• Offers articles, videos, and battlefield preservation efforts, including for Fort Wagner.

3. **Massachusetts Historical Society**[3]

• Home to original letters, photos, and documents relating to the 54th.

4. **BlackPast.org**[4]

• Detailed entries on both the regiment and the broader context of Black American military service.

5. **Civil War Soldiers and Sailors System (CWSS)**

• Search for specific soldiers from the 54th or regimental records.

---

1. https://www.nps.gov/

2. https://www.battlefields.org/

3. https://www.masshist.org/

4. https://www.blackpast.org/

◈ Films & Documentaries

1. *Glory* **(1989)**

• A Hollywood dramatization of the 54th, starring Denzel Washington and Morgan Freeman. While fictionalized, it is grounded in historical fact and inspired renewed interest in the regiment.

2. *The Civil War* **by Ken Burns (1990)** – PBS

• Features segments on the 54th and Fort Wagner with archival visuals and powerful narration.

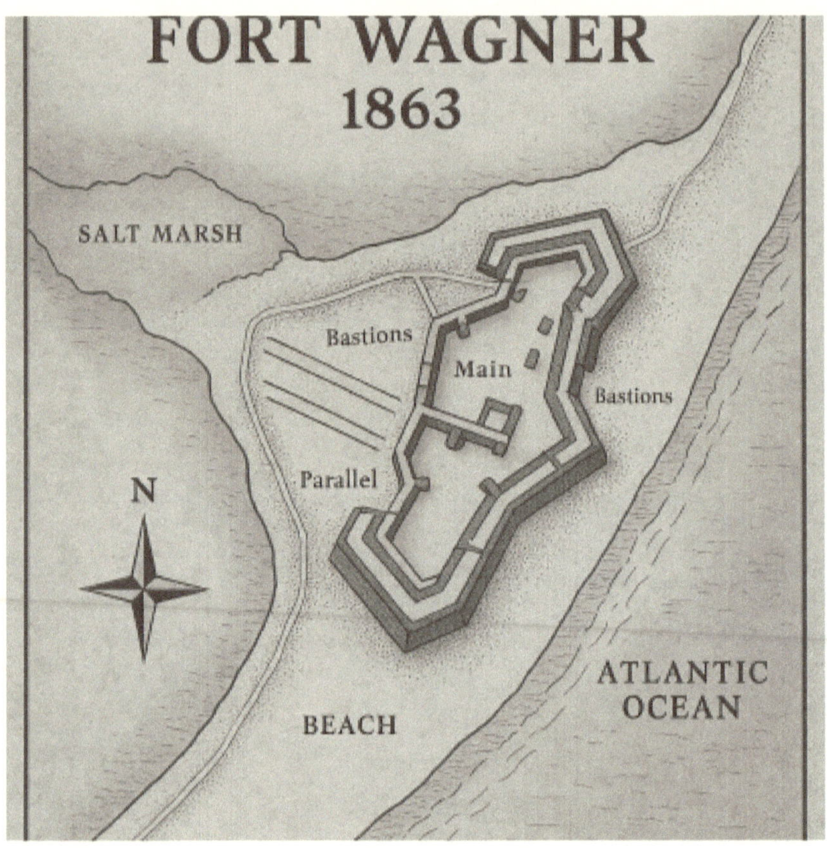

FORT WAGNER
1863
SALT MARSH
Bastions
Main
Bastions
N
Parallel
BEACH
ATLANTIC
OCEAN

◈ Historic Sites & Memorials

1. **Robert Gould Shaw and 54th Regiment Memorial** – Boston Common, Boston, MA

- A stunning bronze relief by Augustus Saint-Gaudens honoring the 54th.

2. **Fort Wagner (Morris Island, SC)**

- **Though eroded by time and tides, the site remains a symbol of Black American valor. Accessible via virtual tours and historical markers.**

Also Coming Soon

Powerstar: Earth's Mightiest Hero
(Paperback Reprint)

THE ATTACK ON FORT WAGNER—THE STORMERS ADVANCING UNDER FIRE

FORT WAGNER: A SOLDIER'S STORY

MARK W LESLIE

This Book is Dedicated to all the Black Men that served during the American Civil War, Many of their names has been lost due to miss management, or uncaring record keeping, and lost of their stories not being told. As a People we should honored them for the bold sacrifice they made for our freedom. As a Country they should be honored for their bold sacrifice for the protecting our Nation.

copyrights

FORT WAGNER: A SOLDIER'S STORY

Don't miss out!

Visit the website below and you can sign up to receive emails whenever Mark W Leslie publishes a new book. There's no charge and no obligation.

https://books2read.com/r/B-A-YTQY-RMSMG

BOOKS 2 READ

Connecting independent readers to independent writers.